ISLINGTON

Please return this item on or before the last date stamped below or you may be liable to overdue charges. To renew an item call the number below, or access the online catalogue at www.islington.gov.uk/libraries. You will need your library membership number and PIN number.

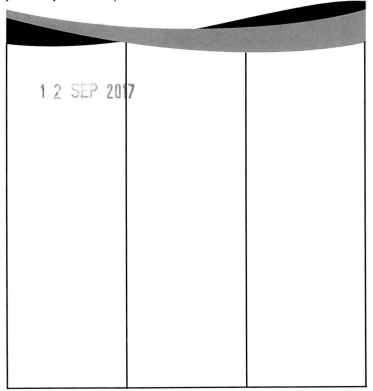

1 2 SEP 2017

Islington Libraries

020 7527 6900   **www.islington.gov.uk/libraries**

Bear Grylls

SURVIVAL SKILLS HANDBOOK

TRACKING

Bear Grylls

This survival handbook has been specially put together to help young adventurers just like you to stay safe in the wild. There's nothing quite like watching animals in their natural habitat, but tracking animals isn't easy. For this, you'll need to hone your detective skills. Learn how to stay hidden in the wild, identify animals from their footprints, and heighten your senses to become the best animal detective. Enjoy the adventure!

Bear

CONTENTS

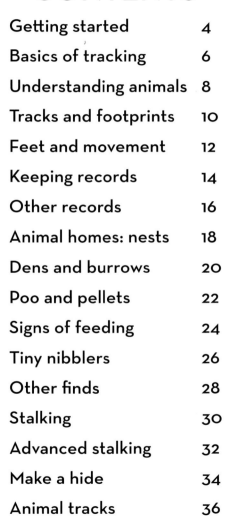

GETTING STARTED

Tracking is the art of detecting animals from the clues they leave behind. This ancient skill allows you to experience the natural world as never before. In a real-life survival situation, you need tracking skills to stay alive!

Ancient craft

In prehistoric times, our ancestors were skilled trackers who survived by hunting animals. In some parts of the world, hunter-gatherers still track animals today.

Survival skills

Survivors of disasters such as plane crashes use tracking skills to find food to stay alive.

Sensing danger

Tracking skills can alert you to dangers in the wild. Rodent or insect tracks show you need to store food out of the reach of animals. Tracks of large animals such as bears show you need to be very wary!

Tune in to nature

It takes patience to become an expert tracker, but the rewards are great. As you become skilled, you will be able to detect animals in the wild and even in parks and cities.

Clothing

Prepare for all sorts of weather on tracking expeditions. You will often be moving slowly, so bring an extra layer of clothing, and cover up if the sun is hot. You will need a warm hat or sunhat, cagoule, gloves, sweater, several layers of clothing, and boots or walking shoes. Take these with you on expeditions: a drink and snack, sunscreen, first aid pouch, torch, and mobile phone. A sit mat can also be useful.

BEAR SAYS

Always tell someone where you are headed when you go tracking. You can always send a text or leave a note.

Equipment

These items of kit are useful for tracking: notebook, pen/pencil, binoculars, magnifying glass, camera, ruler or tape measure, sealable plastic bags for collecting samples, tweezers, torch.

BASICS OF TRACKING

Tracking is about becoming aware of your environment. Animals have keen senses. To become an expert tracker, you need to fully use your senses too.

Sight is the most important sense for humans. Train yourself to notice small details and traces of animals.

Scent can alert you to the presence of animals, and tell you whether clues, such as droppings, are fresh.

Hearing Listen out for bird and animal calls, and sounds such as splashing, crashing, and rustling leaves.

Touch tells you which way the wind is blowing. Feeling the texture of hair and wool can help you identify animals.

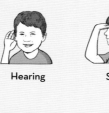

Hearing · Sight

Touch

Scent

BEAR SAYS

Develop night vision by allowing your eyes time to adjust to darkness. Use your torch as little as possible, or tape clear red film over the glass.

Wide-angle vision

Many animals have eyes set far back on their head. This gives a wide field of vision, so they can spot danger from all sides.

Broaden your vision

Develop wide-angle vision in an open space. Hold your arms out in front of you. Scan the area between your hands. Move your arms wider apart and scan again. Keep moving your arms apart to increase your field of view.

Train your hearing

Small sounds such as squeaks and grunts can reveal hidden animals. Ask a friend to hide a wristwatch in a room at night. Train your hearing by following the ticking to find the watch.

Hone your observation

Train your powers of observation by playing this memory game. Ask a friend to put a collection of small objects on a tray, and cover with a cloth. Remove the cloth for a minute and memorise the objects. Replace the cloth. How many objects can you remember?

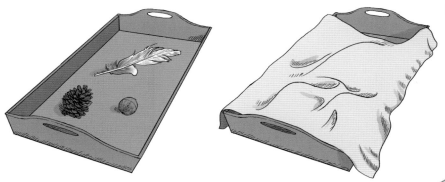

UNDERSTANDING ANIMALS

To track animals effectively you need to understand their needs and put yourself in their position. Expert trackers can work out what an animal was doing from just its track.

Fight for survival

Wild animals face a daily struggle for survival. They must find food and water while avoiding enemies. For a species to survive, animals must breed.

mammals look after their young until they are able to look after themselves

Migration

Animals such as caribou travel on long, regular journeys called migrations. They migrate to find food, avoid cold, or reach a safe place to rear their young. Many birds migrate.

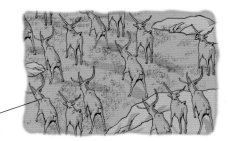

caribou migrate in large groups for extra protection

Water

Almost all animals need to drink clean water daily. Desert animals travel a long way to reach water.

any area with plenty water is a good place to look for wildlife

Food and feeding

Animals have varied feeding habits. Deer, antelope, and rabbits are herbivores, or plant-eaters. Carnivores such as leopards hunt other animals for food. Shrews and hedgehogs are insectivores, or insect-eaters. Bears and pigs are omnivores – they eat a variety of foods.

Habitats

All animals are suited to their habitat. Penguins could not survive in a woodland, and woodland animals would die in Antarctica. Knowing which animals live in local habitats will help you to identify tracks.

Daily rhythms

Animals such as grey squirrels are diurnal – mainly active by day. Nocturnal creatures such as raccoons find food at dawn, dusk, or under cover of night.

Senses

Animal senses are tuned to their way of life and habitat. Cats have night good vision and keen scent and hearing. Touch-sensitive whiskers help them to hunt at night.

Range

Animals such as wolves are widespread. Wolves live on the tundra and in forests, mountains, and other wild places throughout the northern hemisphere.

TRACKS AND FOOTPRINTS

Expert trackers are skilled detectives. The smallest clues provide vital evidence. Trails and footprints are two of the main types of evidence that animals are around.

Where to look

Animal tracks show up best in muddy banks of streams, rivers, lakes, and ponds as well as on damp sand on the seashore. Soft, dusty ground and freshly fallen snow also show up trail marks. If claw-marks are clearly visible, the prints are likely to be fresh.

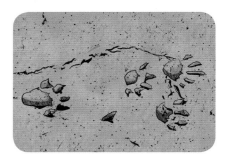

otter pawprint

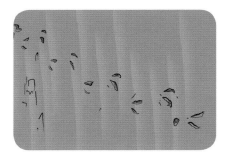

gull print

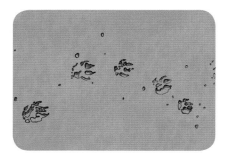

lion pawprint in dust

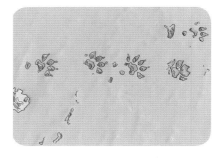

wolverine print in snow

Animal trails

Animals wear paths along regularly used routes, for example from the den to a favoured feeding spot. Look for these trails through woods or long grass, particularly near gaps in fences. Note that trails may be used by more than one animal.

grass bent in one direction shows which way the animal was headed

where deer cross a road, they leave a trail of soil and leaves on the tarmac

deer nibble bark and leaves at head height. This creates a strip bare of vegetation, called a browse line

FEET AND MOVEMENT

Animal feet vary greatly according to species. Animals also move in different ways, leaving distinctive tracks which help to identify species.

Mammal feet
Mammal feet come in different shapes.

Dogs, cats, and foxes have neat, rounded paws which leave rounded prints.

In deer and cattle, two toes have evolved into a cloven (split) hoof. The print is called a slot.

Horses walk on just one toe, which has evolved into a hoof.

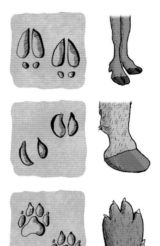

Touching the ground
Bears, badgers, otters, shrews, and hedgehogs walk on the soles of their feet. The print is of the whole foot.

Dogs, cats, and foxes walk and run on their toes. The print shows toe pads but not the heel.

Gait

Animals also move at different speeds. Each gait leaves a distinctive track.

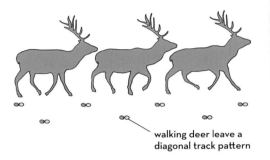

walking deer leave a diagonal track pattern

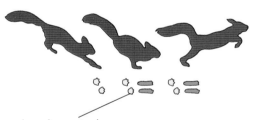

bounding squirrels leave a distinctive track

Bounding

Squirrels, hares, and weasels bound rather than run. The hind and front feet contact the ground alternately.

Bird prints

Birds' feet may be slender, webbed, or lobed. Most birds have three toes pointing forward and one backwards. Birds move in different ways: songbirds hop, pigeons and pheasants walk, while ducks and geese waddle.

KEEPING RECORDS

Keep a record of all the tracks and clues you find in a notebook or journal. Your notes, sketches, and photos build up into an amazing picture of wildlife in your area.

Tracking journal

This sample page shows how to keep records in a notebook.

describe the find and take measurements. Add a sketch or photo. A careful drawing is often clearer than a photo, because you can show details clearly, and leave out any debris that's not part of the print

note the date, time, location, and conditions

can you identify the animal? What do you think it was doing?

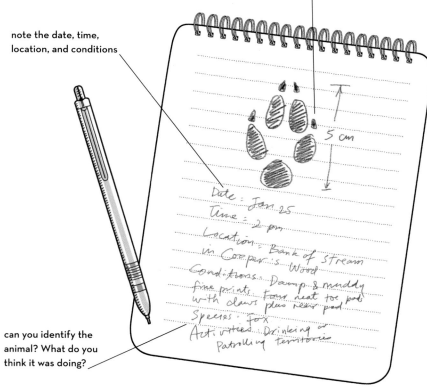

Date: Jan 25
Time: 2 pm
Location: Bank of stream
in Cooper's Wood
Conditions: Damp & muddy
fine prints, four neat toe pad
with claws plus rear pad
Species: Fox
Activities: Drinking or
patrolling territories

5 cm

Taking measurements

Use a ruler or tape measure to record the length and width of prints. Use a tape measure to record stride length and then the width of the animal trail.

Tracking stick

You can use a tracking stick to record animal tracks. All you need is a straight stick and a few elastic bands. Place one end of the stick level with the top of the print. Slide an elastic band down the stick to mark the heel. Use more bands to record the stride length and the trail width. You can also use a marker pen instead of elastic bands.

BEAR SAYS

Use resealable plastic bags to collect finds such as bones, hair, and feathers. Add paper labels to identify your finds.

OTHER RECORDS

Plaster casts and tracings provide an excellent record of the prints you find. Make a tracking bed to record perfect prints.

Make a plaster cast

YOU WILL NEED:

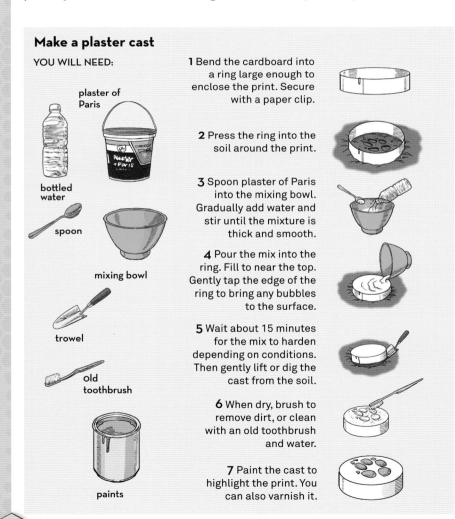

plaster of Paris

bottled water

spoon

mixing bowl

trowel

old toothbrush

paints

1 Bend the cardboard into a ring large enough to enclose the print. Secure with a paper clip.

2 Press the ring into the soil around the print.

3 Spoon plaster of Paris into the mixing bowl. Gradually add water and stir until the mixture is thick and smooth.

4 Pour the mix into the ring. Fill to near the top. Gently tap the edge of the ring to bring any bubbles to the surface.

5 Wait about 15 minutes for the mix to harden depending on conditions. Then gently lift or dig the cast from the soil.

6 When dry, brush to remove dirt, or clean with an old toothbrush and water.

7 Paint the cast to highlight the print. You can also varnish it.

Make tracings

You need a clear sheet of acetate and a permanent marker pen. Place the acetate over the print and carefully trace the outline with the pen.

Alternatively, you can use a non-permanent marker to trace onto a small piece of Perspex. Scan or copy the drawing then wipe clean and use again.

Make a tracking bed

Make a tracking bed near an animal burrow by clearing loose twigs, stones and leaves away. Smooth the ground flat with the edge of a ruler. Return the next day to find a clear set of prints.

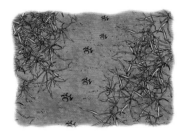

Make a tracking bed

Make a tracking bed in your backyard by sprinkling sand onto a tray to a depth of about 3 cm. Smooth flat with the edge of a ruler. You could put a spoonful of dog or cat food in the centre to act as bait. Leave overnight and check the next day.

ANIMAL HOMES: NESTS

Birds build nests in spring to rear their young. Each species builds a characteristic shape. Mammals such as squirrels and dormice also make nests.

What's it made of?

Birds use different materials to build their nests. Shape, structure, and materials all help to identify nest-builders.

Warning sign: Never approach birds' nests in spring and summer, when they may contain eggs or young.

BEAR SAYS

Size is an obvious clue as to the identity of nest-builders. The bigger the bird or animal, the larger the nest.

woodpeckers

storks

wood pigeons

coots

kingfishers

ringed plovers

1 Songbirds weave twigs into a cup-shaped nest. Thrushes line their nests with mud.

2 Wrens build ball-shaped nests with a small, round entrance hole. Long-tailed tits build similar nests made of moss and lichen bound with cobwebs.

3 Wood pigeons build loose, untidy nests of sticks.

4 Rooks nest high in a clump of trees. The nest colony is called a rookery.

5 Storks build large, untidy stick nests perched on chimneys.

6 Peregrine falcons nest on crags and church steeples.

7 Kingfishers nest in holes along the river bank.

8 Swallows build nests of mud and saliva under the eaves of houses.

9 Coots and grebes build floating nests of vegetation.

10 Ringed plovers nest in hollow scrapes on the beach. Their eggs resemble pebbles.

11 Woodpeckers chisel out nest holes in tree trunks using their sharp beaks.

12 A squirrel nest, called a drey, is built into the crook of a tree.

13 Dormice nest in tree holes lined with fresh leaves.

peregrine falcons

squirrels

songbirds (thrushes)

rooks

swallows

wrens

DENS AND BURROWS

Mammals such as foxes and badgers shelter underground in dens and burrows. It's not always easy to identify who is living underground. Many insects, some reptiles, and even birds live in burrows too.

badger sett

BEAR SAYS

Droppings and food scraps near the burrow can help to identify the owner. The size of entrance holes provides another clue.

bear den

hare form

prairie dog burrow

1 A fox's den is called an earth. Smelly droppings and bones mark the entrance.

2 A badger's den is called a sett. This underground home has several chambers. A large heap of earth marks the entrance. Badgers sharpen their claws on a nearby tree.

3 A rabbit warren contains a network of tunnels. Look for small, round droppings and nibbled grass near entrance holes.

4 Hares shelter above ground in grassy hollows. This hidden home is called a form.

5 Bears hibernate in rocky caves or hollow trees in winter. Never approach a bear's den.

6 Mole hills of excavated earth show where a mole lives underground.

7 A prairie dog colony has many chambers linked by tunnels. Burrowing owls, ferrets, and rattlesnakes may move into these burrows.

8 A squiggly heap called a worm cast marks the entrance to an earthworm's burrow. The heap is made of undigested soil that has passed through the worm's body.

9 The nests of meadow ants create grassy mounds in open pasture.

10 Wood ants nest in large mounds of pine needles in woodlands.

rabbit warren

mole hills

meadow ant mound

worm cast

fox den (earth)

wood ant nest

POO AND PELLETS

Animal poo or scat is another sure sign that animals are about. Look closely and you may see evidence of what the animal has been eating. Skilled trackers can identify animals from their scat.

Whose poo?

Animals produce droppings of different shapes. Droppings contain dangerous bacteria so never touch them with your hands – use a stick to if you want to investigate. Always wash hands thoroughly after any contact with poo, or wipe with a moist tissue.

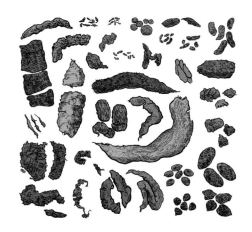

Animals such as foxes, otters, and badgers use dung and urine to mark their territories. Badgers dig small holes called latrines. Otters leave their scat, called spraint, in an obvious place such as on a large stone.

Pellets

Birds of prey cannot digest the fur and bones of their prey. They cough up these remains as pellets. Bits of fur and bones provide clues about the predator's diet.

BEAR SAYS

Are the droppings fresh? Fresh dung is moist and attracts flies. As time goes on, droppings decay or dry out.

Size and shape

Different bird species produce pellets of different shapes, sizes, and colours.

Dissect an owl pellet

Pellets can be dissected to find out what the bird has been eating.

1 Soak the pellet in a tray filled with water for at least an hour. Add a few drops of disinfectant to the water.

2 Tease the pellet apart using tweezers. Separate the bones and clean them in a disinfectant solution.

3 Sort and arrange the bones into skulls, limb bones, ribs, etc. Can you identify the owl's prey?

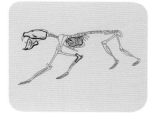

SIGNS OF FEEDING

Animals leave debris as they feed. These leftovers can give away their whereabouts. Nibbled vegetation shows the presence of plant-eaters, while predators leave the remains of kills.

Nibbled nuts

Birds, rodents, and squirrels all eat nuts. Mice nibble small, neat holes in shells. Woodpeckers and nuthatches wedge nuts into tree bark to open them with their bills. Squirrels bury nuts to eat later – a behaviour called caching.

Grass and leaves

Rabbits and rodents snip plant stems using sharp front teeth called incisors, leaving neatly sliced edges.
Deer lack incisors so they leave frayed edges as they strip twigs and bark.

Thrush's anvil

Thrushes smash snails against stones to reach the soft molluscs inside.

Pine cones

Squirrels and some birds eat pine seeds. Crossbills pluck the seeds, leaving cones with ragged edges. Squirrels strip pinecones to the stalk.

Beaver damage

Beavers gnaw through saplings to build their underwater home, called a lodge.

Bird kill

Tufts of feathers mark the spot where a hawk has killed a songbird.

Rooting boars

Boars and pigs leave a line of debris as they dig beneath the grass for roots and fungi.

Sap sucker

Woodpeckers leave a line of holes in trees as they dig for sap below the bark.

TINY NIBBLERS

Nibbled leaves, holes in wood, and other debris mark where insects and other minibeasts have been feeding.

Leaf damage

Caterpillars are hungry feeders! Some species nibble large holes in leaves, others munch inward from the edges. Some fly, and beetle larvae "mine" leaves from the inside, leaving a pale trail.

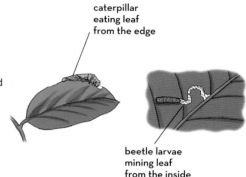

caterpillar
eating leaf
from the edge

beetle larvae
mining leaf
from the inside

Ant trails

Look for ant trails leading from the nest to a food source such as fruit or an injured minibeast. Watch the insects scurry to and fro along the trail. Can you see what they are carrying back to the nest?
Tropical leafcutter ants snip leaves to carry back to their nest.

Galls

Some wasps and flies lay their eggs in buds, which provide food for the larvae. The plant defends itself by forming a growth called a gall around the insect.

Woodborers

Some beetles lay their eggs in dead wood or lumber. The grubs eat their way through the timber and then fly away as adults, leaving exit holes in the wood.

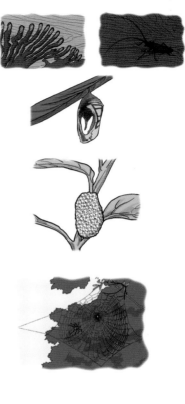

Butterfly pupa

Young butterflies pass through a pupa (chrysalis) stage as they change from larvae into adults. You may find a pupa case hanging from a leaf or twig by a silken thread.

Cuckoo spit

This unpleasant-looking blob of foam hides a young insect called a froghopper nymph as it sucks sap from plant stems.

Spider webs

Spiders spin silken webs to trap their victims. Look closely to see prey such as woodlice tied up with silk.

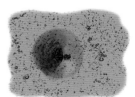

Antlion pit

Young insects called antlions dig cone-shaped pits and hide at the bottom. Ants slide down the steep sides into the insect's jaws.

BEAR SAYS

Use a magnifying glass to get a close-up view of clues such as nibbled leaves. Shine a torch behind a mined leaf with to highlight the young insect's trail.

OTHER FINDS

From time to time, keen-eyed trackers will come across finds such as bones, shells, and feathers. These provide clues about animal anatomy and their way of life.

Skulls

Skulls and other bones can tell you a lot about body structure. Field guides and online sites help to identify species. The shape and size of teeth and jaws reveal an animal's diet.

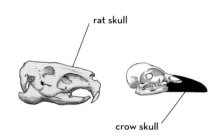

rat skull

crow skull

fox skull

Feathers

Birds moult their plumage at least once a year. Again, online sources and field guides can help to identify the species.

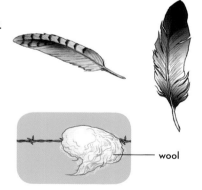

Hair and wool

Hair caught on barbed wire shows where animals pass regularly. You may also find the remains of livestock such as wool.

wool

hair

Wing print
A wing print in the snow shows where a
bird escaped a predator such as a fox.

Moulted skins
Reptiles, insects, and woodlice moult their
skins as they grow. Snakes shed their skin
in one piece. This is called sloughing.
A dragonfly climbs out of its case to
become an adult insect.

By the sea
Shells on the shore are the remains of
marine molluscs. This holed shell has been
pierced by a predatory mollusc called a
whelk. This leathery "mermaid's purse"
is the egg case of a dogfish.

Eggshells
Baby birds that hatch naturally usually
leave a shell in two neat halves.
A ragged hole pecked from the outside is
the work of a predator.

Dung ball
Dung beetles roll cattle dung into
neat balls and lay their eggs inside.

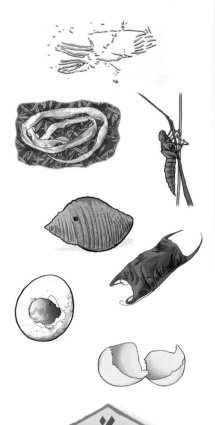

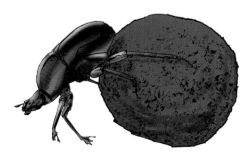

BEAR SAYS
The shape of the skul provides
clues about the animal species.
Wearing gloves, clean bones
with an old toothbrush and
disinfectant solution.

STALKING

Stalking is the art of watching animals without being noticed by them. Remember, animals are always on the alert for danger, so avoiding detection takes a lot of skill.

Camouflage

Wear clothing that blends in with your surroundings. If you don't have army-style camouflage, wear natural colours such as greens and browns. Avoid bright colours. Patterns or patches help to break up your outline.

make sure to camouflage your skin

Skin camouflage

Pale human skin stands out in nature. Smear stripes of mud onto exposed skin such as face and hands, or use charred wood from a campfire.

Using binoculars

Keep shiny objects such as camera and binoculars hidden under your jacket, with the strap round your neck. When you need to use binoculars, raise them slowly to your face, keeping your eyes on the target. Avoid sudden movements.

Outline and shadow

Animals can easily detect the human outline and shadow. Disguise your outline with leafy twigs or ivy. Avoid casting a shadow on small creatures such as insects.

Silhouette

Your outline stands out clearly silhouetted against the skyline. Keep low or hide behind cover. Water creatures will spot you immediately if you peer over the bank of a pond or stream.

Using cover

Shrubs and trees provide good cover for watching wildlife. If you have to move through open ground, crawl or crouch low, and use long grass, ditches, or hollows as cover.

BEAR SAYS

The best way to avoid detection is to keep very still and quiet. Find a spot behind cover and be patient. A foam mat will keep you comfortable while waiting.

ADVANCED STALKING

Predators use stealth to approach their prey, creeping forward while keeping to cover. You can use similar techniques to get close to wildlife without being seen.

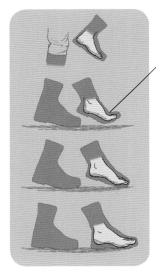

carefully test the ground with the balls of your feet

Fox walk

Advance slowly and carefully. With your weight on you back foot, place the ball of your front foot down, testing for twigs or dry leaves that might crack or rustle. If the ground is clear, move your weight forward onto your front foot. Repeat. Advance just a few paces then stop, listen and look around you. Avoid sudden movements.

Freezing

If you are spotted, freeze. If you keep quite still, animals may not be able to spot you, or will see you as less of a threat.

Leopard crawl

Use this crawl to move through long grass. Get down on all fours with your weight on your knees and forearms. Move your right elbow and left knee at the same time, then the opposite pair.

Stomach crawl

Use this crawl in open ground. Lie on your stomach with your arms out in front and legs splayed behind. Move forward by pulling with your forearms while pushing with the inside of your feet.

Moving downwind

Your scent will give you away if you approach animals upwind, with the wind blowing your scent towards them. Test wind direction by licking one finger and holding it up in the breeze. Or drop a few grass stems to see which way they blow. Circle around at a distance until you are downwind of your target.

BEAR SAYS

If you spot an animal, don't try to get too close – watch at a distance. If it moves off, don't follow quickly. After you have finished watching, move away quietly.

MAKE A HIDE

A hide will conceal you while you watch wildlife. Set up your hide near a den or burrow, where many tracks cross, or by a stream where animals drink.

You need: 5–6 canes, camouflaged tarpaulin, string, tent pegs

camouflage a plain tarpaulin by sewing patches of brown or green cloth onto a plain one. Ask adult permission first

Tepee hide

1 Tie the canes loosely at one end with string. Fan out the other ends to make a cone shape. Press the canes into the ground.

2 Drape the tarpaulin around the tepee shape. Fasten the opening with safety pins or by looping string through the eyeholes. Leave a gap at eye height for wildlife watching.

3 Peg the tarp down or weight down the edges with stones or branches. Add a stool or mat inside for comfort.

4 Camouflage the outside with leaves, ivy, or branches.

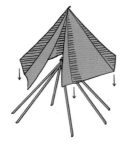

Camouflaged A-frame

1 You can also rig a camouflaged tarp as an A-frame shelter. You need a length of cord. Tie one end of the cord to a tree at a height of about 80 cm. Peg the other end to the ground so the cord is tight.

2 Drape the tarp over the cord. Fold any spare material underneath to act as a groundsheet. Peg or weight the edges down with stones or branches. Use branches to disguise the entrance, leaving a gap to observe wildlife.

BEAR SAYS

Research animal behaviour and choose the right time for your stakeout. If animals emerge at dusk, get into position at least half an hour before. Sit tight and your

ANIMAL TRACKS: CARNIVORES

The mammal group called carnivores includes dogs, cats, foxes, weasels, and badgers. All of these animals are meat-eating predators that hunt other animals for food.

Domestic dog F 5–10 cm; H 5–10 cm
Range: worldwide except Antarctic
Habitat: with humans
Diet: varied, including meat, scraps

Wolf F 10–11 cm; H 10–11 cm
Range: North America, Europe, Asia
Habitat: forest, grassland, desert, tundra
Diet: mammals including deer, hares, rodents

Coyote F 6 cm; H 5 cm
Range: North America
Habitat: forest, grassland, desert
Diet: rabbits, rodents, reptiles, insects, fruit

Red fox F 5 cm; H 5 cm
Range: North America, Europe, Asia, introduced to Australia
Habitat: forests, grassland, mountains, deserts, cities
Diet: small mammals, birds, insects, scraps

Domestic cat F 2.5–5 cm; H 2.5–5 cm
Range: worldwide except Arctic and Antarctic
Habitat: with humans
Diet: meat

Lynx F 10–11 cm; H 7 cm
Range: Europe, Asia, North America
Habitat: forest
Diet: hares, rodents, birds

Brown bear F 23–30 cm; H 23–30 cm.
Range: North America, Europe, Asia
Habitat: forests, mountains, tundra
Diet: fish, carrion, berries, vegetation, insects, fungi, rodents, sheep

Striped skunk F 5 cm; H 5 cm
Range: North America
Habitat: woods, grasslands, deserts, cities
Diet: insects, worms, reptiles, amphibians, birds, eggs, berries, leaves

Racoon F 5 cm; H 10 cm
Range: North and Central America
Habitat: woods, grasslands, mountains, near water, urban
Diet: insects, worms, fruit, nuts, fish, amphibians, eggs

American opossum F 27 cm; H 5 cm
Range: North, Central and South America
Habitat: woodlands, brush, near water
Diet: insects, amphibians, carrion, small birds and mammals, eggs, berries, plants

European badger F 6–7 cm; H 6–7 cm
Range: Europe, western Asia
Habitat: woodland, meadows, urban
Diet: worms, insects, amphibians, fruit, grain, small mammals, birds

Stoat F 2 cm; H 3.5 cm
Range: North America, Europe, Asia, introduced to New Zealand
Habitat: woods, grassland, moorland
Diet: rodents, rabbits, shrews, birds, fish

BROWERS AND GRAZERS

Deer, cattle, sheep, and horses all belong to a group of mammals called ungulates. Deer, cattle, and sheep have cloven hooves. In horses, just one toe has evolved into a hoof. All are plant-eaters, as are marsupials such as kangaroos.

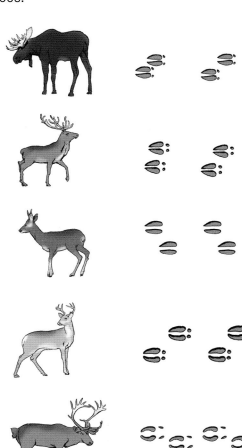

Moose/Elk F 11–15 cm; H 11–15 cm
Range: North America, Europe, Asia
Habitat: marsh, woodland
Diet: leaves, twigs, moss, water plants

Red deer F 7–8 cm; H 7–8 cm
Range: Europe, Northwest Africa, Asia, introduced Australia, New Zealand, South America
Habitat: grassland, woodland, moor
Diet: grass, plants, heather

Roe deer F 5 cm; H 5 cm
Range: Europe, western Asia, introduced to Australia
Habitat: woodland, grassland
Diet: grass, leaves, shoots, berries

White-tailed deer F 7.5 cm; H 6.5 cm
Range: North, Central and South America
Habitat: woodland, scrub
Diet: grass, shrub, fungi, lichen, nuts

Caribou/Reindeer F 10 cm; H 10 cm
Range: North America, Scandinavia, north Asia
Habitat: tundra, forests, mountains
Diet: plants, leaves, twigs, lichen

Muntjac F 2.5–3 cm; H 2.5–3 cm
Range: Asia, introduced UK
Habitat: forests, farmland
Diet: grass, leaves, shoots

Cattle F 10 cm; H 10 cm
Range: every continent except Antarctica and Arctic
Habitat: farmland, meadows
Diet: grasses

Sheep F 6 cm; H 6 cm
Range: every continent except Antarctica and Arctic
Habitat: farmland, moors, scrub
Diet: grasses, plants

Horse
Range: every continent except Antarctica and Arctic
Habitat: farmland, grasslands, mountains
Diet: grasses, grain

Wild boar F, H 12 cm including dewclaws
Range: Europe, North Africa, Asia
Habitat: forests, scrub
Diet: leaves, roots, fungi, small mammals, reptiles, carrion, eggs, manure

Red kangaroo
Range: Australia
Habitat: grassland and scrub
Diet: grass

Numbat
Range: Australia
Habitat: eucalyptus woodlands
Diet: termites, ants

SMALL MAMMALS

Rodents such as rats, mice, and squirrels nibble plant food using chisel-like front teeth called incisors. Rabbits and hares also have incisors. Shrews and hedgehogs hunt insects. They are rarely seen but you sometimes find their tracks.

Brown rat F 1 cm; H 2.5 cm
Range: every continent except Antarctica
Habitat: near water or humans
Diet: seeds, grains, many other foods

House mouse F 0.6 cm; H 0.6 cm
Range: worldwide
Habitat: near humans
Diet: seeds, grains, fruit, meat

European rabbit F 2.5 cm; H 6 cm
Range: Europe, North Africa, introduced to Australia
Habitat: grassland, farmland, scrub
Diet: grass, twigs, bark, crop plants

Brown hare F 4 cm; H 6–15 cm
Range: Europe, Asia
Habitat: dry grasslands
Diet: grass, plants, twigs, bark

Jackrabbit F 4 cm; H 10 cm
Range: western North America
Habitat: grasslands and farmland
Diet: grass

Grey Squirrel F 4–5 cm; H 5–6 cm
Range: North America, introduced to Europe
Habitat: woodlands, urban
Diet: nuts, flowers, buds

Prairie dog F 3 cm; H 4 cm
Range: North and Central America
Habitat: grasslands
Diet: wood, bark, pine needles, buds, roots,
seeds, leaves

Alpine marmot
Range: Europe
Habitat: mountains
Diet: grasses, grain, insects, spiders, worms

North American porcupine F 7 cm; H 8 cm
Range: North America
Habitat: forest, brush
Diet: wood, bark, pine needles, buds, roots,
seeds, leaves

Common shrew F 0.5 cm; H 1.5 cm
Range: Europe
Habitat: woodland, grassland, hedges
Diet: insects, slugs, spiders, worms,
amphibians, small rodents

Hedgehog F 5 cm; H 5 cm
Range: Europe, northwest Asia
Habitat: woods, grassland, gardens
Diet: insects, slugs, fish, frogs, worms, baby
mice, birds

BIRDS

Birds come in many sizes, from hummingbirds to ostriches. They have very different tracks because their feet are suited to their habitat. They also move in different ways, whether hopping, walking, or running.

House sparrow 2 cm
Range: worldwide
Habitat: urban and farmland
Diet: seeds, plants, insects, worms

Song thrush
Range: Europe, Asia, North Africa, introduced Australia, New Zealand
Habitat: woodlands, gardens
Diet: snails, slugs, insects, worms, fruit, berries

Raven 5 cm
Range: North America, Europe, Asia, North Africa
Habitat: open country
Diet: rodents, invertebrates, carrion

Wood pigeon 5 cm
Range: Europe, Asia, North Africa
Habitat: woodlands
Diet: seeds, plants, invertebrates

Common pheasant 6 cm
Range: Europe, Asia, introduced North America, Australia, New Zealand
Habitat: woodland
Diet: seeds, plants, berries, invertebrates

Turkey 10 cm
Range: North America and introduced worldwide except Antarctica as farm stock
Habitat: woodland, farms
Diet: seeds, berries, nuts, invertebrates

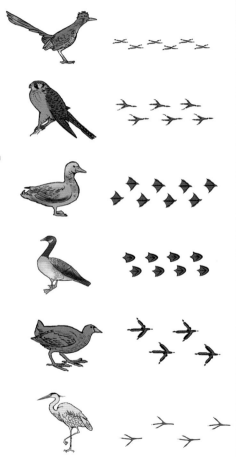

Roadrunner 7.5 cm
Range: North America
Habitat: open country, desert
Diet: insects, lizards, snakes

Sparrowhawk
Range: Europe, Asia, North Africa
Habitat: woodland
Diet: woodland birds

Mallard duck 5 cm
Range: North America, Europe, Asia, North
Africa, introduced Australia, New Zealand
Habitat: near freshwater and coasts
Diet: plants, snails, insects,
crustaceans, worms

Canada goose 7.5 cm
Range: North America, Europe, Asia
Habitat: near water
Diet: plants

Coot 4 cm
Range: Europe, Asia, North Africa,
introduced Australia, New Zealand
Habitat: near fresh water
Diet: algae, plants, seeds, fruit, small
animals, eggs

Grey heron 10 cm
Range: Europe, Asia, North Africa
Habitat: near water
Diet: fish and other water creatures

BY WATER

Animal tracks show up clearly on sandy seashores and along the muddy banks of streams, lakes and rivers. A wide variety of birds, mammals, reptiles, and other small creatures live here.

On the seashore

Herring gull
Range: coasts worldwide
Habitat: coasts and inland
Diet: carrion, eggs, fish, crustaceans, many other foods

Eurasian Oystercatcher
Range: coasts of Europe and Asia
Habitat: tidal mudflats
Diet: small crustaceans and other invertebrates

Common seal
Range: North Atlantic, Pacific and Arctic coasts
Habitat: sheltered coastal waters
Diet: fish, squid, crustaceans

Green turtle
Range: tropical and subtropical oceans
Habitat: marine, lay eggs on sandy beaches
Diet: jellyfish, fish eggs, worm, sponges, algae, crustaceans

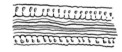

Shore crab
Range: coasts worldwide
Habitat: coastal waters
Diet: molluscs, worms, crustaceans

Lugworm
Range: coasts of Europe and North America
Habitat: sandy seashore
Diet: decaying creatures in sand

By fresh water

Eurasian otter F 6.5 cm; H 7 cm
Range: Europe, Asia, North Africa
Habitat: lakes, streams, rivers
Diet: fish, crustaceans, amphibians, insects, birds

American beaver F 5 cm; H 15 cm
Range: North America
Habitat: streams, small lakes
Diet: wood, leaves, roots, bark

American mink F 3.5 cm; H 4 cm
Range: North America, introduced to Europe
Habitat: swamps, near streams and lakes
Diet: fish, amphibians, small mammals, crayfish

Water vole F 2 cm; H 2 cm
Range: Europe, Asia
Habitat: banks of streams and rivers
Diet: grasses, rushes

European common frog
Range: Europe
Habitat: near water in meadows, woods, gardens
Diet: insects, snails, worms, tadpoles, algae

American crocodile
Range: North, Central and South America
Habitat: rivers and estuaries
Diet: fish, turtles, birds

GLOSSARY

Caching When an animal hides food to eat later.

Canine A member of the dog family; also the pointed teeth of carnivorous animals, that are used for seizing prey.

Carnivore An animal that eats meat. Carnivores are also a group of meat-eating mammals that includes dogs, cats, foxes, and weasels.

Cloven Divided into two. Cattle and deer have cloven (split) hooves.

Diurnal An animal that is active by day.

Drey The nest of a squirrel.

Evolve When an animal species slowly changes in order to suit its changing environment.

Gait A form of movement, such as walking, trotting, or galloping.

Gall A growth made by a tree, shrub, or plant where an insect has laid an egg.

Herbivore An animal that eats plants.

Hibernation When animals enter a deep sleep to survive winter.

Incisor Sharp, chisel-like front teeth.

Insectivore An animal that eats insects.

Invertebrate One of a group of animals such as insects, molluscs, and crustaceans, that lack a backbone.

Larva A young insect, also called a grub or nymph.

Migration When animals go on regular seasonal journeys to avoid cold, find food, or reach a safe place to breed.

Nocturnal An animal that is active by night.

Pellet Indigestible remains coughed up by a bird of prey.

Pupa The "resting" stage of a young insect before it becomes an adult. Also called a chrysalis.

Range The total area in which an animal species lives.

Scat Animal dung or poo.

Slot The print of a cloven-hoofed animal, such as a deer or cow.

Species A particular type of living thing, such as an African elephant.

Ungulate A hoofed mammal, such as sheep and deer.

Webbed The feet of aquatic (water-dwelling) animals such as ducks and otters, which have skin between the toes.

Discover more amazing books in the Bear Grylls series:

Perfect for young adventurers, the *Survival Skills* series accompanies an exciting range of colouring and activity books. Curious kids can also learn tips and tricks for almost any extreme situation in *Survival Camp*, and explore Earth in *Extreme Planet*.

Conceived by Weldon Owen in partnership with Bear Grylls Ventures

Produced by Weldon Owen Ltd
Suite 3.08 The Plaza, 535 King's Road,
London SW10 0SZ, UK

WELDON OWEN LTD
Publisher Donna Gregory
Designer Shahid Mahmood
Editorial Claire Philip, Susie Rae, Lydia Halliday
Illustrators Bernard Chau

10 9 8 7 6 5 4 3 2 1

Disclaimer

Weldon Owen and Bear Grylls take pride in doing our best to get the facts right in putting together the information in this book, but occasionally something slips past our beady eyes. Therefore we make no warranties about the accuracy or completeness of the information in the book and, to the maximum extent permitted, we disclaim all liability. Wherever possible, we will endeavour to correct any errors of fact at reprint.

Kids – if you want to try any of the activities in this book, please ask your parents first! Parents – all outdoor activities carry some degree of risk and we recommend that anyone participating in these activities be aware of the risks involved and seek professional instruction and guidance. None of the health/medical information in this book is intended as a substitute for professional medical advice; always seek the advice of a qualified practitioner.

A WELDON OWEN PRODUCTION. AN IMPRINT OF KINGS ROAD PUBLISHING
PART OF THE BONNIER PUBLISHING GROUP.